The Glory

Its Nature and End-Time Purpose

Michael Major

FIRST EDITION

Maon Publishing
P.O. Box 105
O'Brien, Florida 32071

ISBN 13: 978-0-692-94300-7
ISBN 10: 0692943005

Cover art: "Kingdom Come," graphic and interior format designed by Marie Fowler.

Author website: www.thechabod.com

CONTENTS

DEDICATION

To my beloved wife Sherry and our spiritual daughter Marie Fowler, without whom this book would not have been published.

ACKNOWLEDGEMENTS

For the inspiration of this book, I must first thank my dear friend and mentor, Stephen Gray, a missionary to Muslim East Africa, who first introduced me to the outpouring of God's glory in 2001 and who has faithfully taught and discipled me in my ongoing experience and understanding of it ever since then.

Also, I cannot fail to give particular honorable mention to my beloved wife, Sherry Major, a Jew and daughter of Abraham who lived in Jerusalem, Israel and attended Ruth Ward Heflin's glory meetings mentioned in Ms. Heflin's seminal book, "Glory." My wife greatly contributed to my understanding not only of the Glory itself but also of the pre-eminent importance of Israel in the end-time revelation of God's Glory.

Lastly, I must honor and thank Ruth Ward Heflin herself, albeit posthumously, for her groundbreaking book on this subject, which, at the time it was first published, was virtually the only available teaching in this area from any authoritative source.

ENDORSEMENTS

I met Michael Major when he invited me to speak at his church in Florida. It was amazing how God visited us both so powerfully before the service as we struggled just to enter the church door. God rarely pours out on ministers today. It takes one who is hungry and seeking of God. Michael is such a man, who desires to see God glorified in all that he does. Due to our mutual encounters with the glory of God, we both have seen God do incredible things. Michael truly touches God's heart through his worship and ministers in a powerful anointing. I believe Michael was inspired by God to write about his experience with God's glory and to share his insights. It is rare to read something that reflects a profound experience with God. This book about the glory of God will touch your life and cause your spirit to be impassioned for God. I recommend this book to those who are hungry and seeking of a touch from God -- you won't be disappointed.

-Dr. Stephen L Gray,
Pastor Followers of Christ Fellowship
Florence, AL

Michael Major has written an anointed, revelation-filled book for Christians who are genuinely hungry spiritually and avidly desire to experience the Glory. Within His lengthy prayer hours before the Cross, Jesus promised that this is possible. He prayed, "*Father, I will/ desire that they whom You have given Me, be with Me where I am; that they may behold My glory which Thou has given Me ...* " John 17:24.

Some Christians, perhaps many, believe and testify that they have experienced the Glory when actually what they experienced was the anointing. Michael brings out clearly through the Scriptures that there is a vast difference between the two. I encourage you to read and see the difference which, I believe, can and will revolutionize your Christian walk.

-Retha Garten,
Author and Pastor of North Florida Christian Center

The Glory – Its Nature and End Time Purpose by Michael Major is the most exhaustive and compelling study of God's glory that I have ever read. Truly God is glorified in this book. This is a must read for anyone who wants to understand and experience the glory of God.

-Dr. Jim Guth, Regional Manager,
Billy Graham Evangelistic Association

CHAPTER 1
THE GLORY –HISTORY AND HYPE

Over the past five years or so, the topic of "the Glory" seems to have suddenly become quite popular and ubiquitous among charismatics and Pentecostal Christians. The term is bandied about as freely and widely now as "revival" was in the early nineties, and is similarly taken for granted as an experiential phenomenon. If you were to ask the average evangelical Christian, most would claim to understand the subject of "the Glory" or would have at least formed an opinion about it. Most Christians, particularly of the charismatic or Pentecostal variety, have either sung songs about "the Glory" or have heard this subject referred to in sermons or at conferences, and many claim to minister "in it" or have otherwise boasted of experienced it. Similarly, many churches claim to have experienced "revival" but never have actually witnessed or experienced anything anywhere near as powerful and historic as Azusa Street, Toronto or Brownsville. As with any spiritual experience, however, the beauty is frequently in the eye of the beholder, and, just as "revival" in the nineties was far more widely claimed to have occurred than was actually the case, the same can be said for "the Glory" today. In short, there is a lot of hype and precious little reality which can translate to actual experience and scripturally grounded understanding, not to mention the most precious commodity of all – real and lasting fruit in the lives of believers.

When the phenomenon of the "charismatic movement" first began to take hold in the late 60's and early 70's in America, many Christians assumed that they had some knowledge of the Holy Spirit, at least doctrinally. In those days, however, prior to the advent of Christian TV, the average Christian did not speak in other tongues, experience or minister in divine healing, or have regular contact with the realm of miracles and dramatic supernatural experiences. Yet if you asked the average Christian back then, "have you received the Holy Spirit since you believed?" (Acts 19:2), most would respond "yes" even though there was no evidence of the power of the Holy Spirit in their lives at all.

Virtually no one at that time knew what was meant by "receiving the Holy Spirit" or what it actually meant to have received Him, yet most would claim to know or have experienced the Holy Spirit based on a generalized logical assumption that, well after all, they must have received Him at conversion, so He must be "at work in their lives" in some subjective way. A more genuine response would have been "well, no, actually I don't know what you're talking about" (the response of the disciples at Ephesus in Acts 19:2).

Yet the fact remains that "receiving the Holy Spirit" can be a tangible, documentable phenomenon with powerfully demonstrated effects and results in the lives of believers. This reality is no longer a novelty or subject to debate, because since 1973 and the advent of Christian TV, a wealth of accurate information and experience about the Baptism of the Holy Spirit has poured forth to a worldwide audience, clearly demonstrating what it means, from the standpoint of Acts 19:2, to "have received the Holy Spirit." In short, the gift or baptism of the Holy Spirit was then and is now available to eager and genuinely hungry believers willing to be taught about it. This experience is readily available to those who have admitted to themselves and to others in the Church that they know nothing about it experientially, and who have no pre-conceived ideas about it. Once the experience of the Holy Spirit is received, the fact of this experience is obvious, scripturally verifiable, and can be clearly and powerfully demonstrated both to believers and non-believers alike. You either have it or you don't. And those who have it can demonstrate it "with authority, and not as the Scribes." (Matthew 7:29.) Those who don't, sadly enough, often remain in ignorance and unteachability. You simply cannot receive *what you think you already have.*

The same holds true of the experience of the Glory.

It is available to those who genuinely hunger for it and are willing to admit they know nothing about it. It is there for those who freely acknowledge they have no experience or understanding of it whatsoever, and are willing to be taught. Sadly though, there are not many qualified teachers who have actually experienced the Glory, and a proliferation of folks who claim to have already experienced something they know absolutely nothing about. My experience in the last 10 years has been that most Christians are not willing to be taught about this subject, because they believe they already understand it. As a result, a plethora of ignorance and misunderstanding is pouring forth from those who claim to have experienced "the anointing" and think the "anointing" and the "Glory" are synonymous. *They are most emphatically not* – not in Scripture, nor in the actual experience of those who have genuinely experienced the Glory and are exhibiting its fruit in their lives. Understanding the difference between these two experiences – the "anointing" and the "Glory" – is critical if one is to gain any understanding of the Glory of God and to enter into the experience of it. The question for the Reader is – are you willing to entertain the possibility you do not know what the "Glory" actually is? Are you willing to be taught about it – from "scratch", as it were, so that you may enter into it? Can you abandon pre-conceived notions.?

CHAPTER 2
THE GLORY IN SCRIPTURE

But we should always give thanks to God for you, brethren, beloved by the Lord, because God has chosen you from the beginning for salvation through sanctification by the Spirit and faith in the truth. And it was for this He called you through our gospel, that you may **gain the glory** *of our Lord Jesus Christ.* (II Thessalonians 2:13-14.)

By this scripture we are made to understand that entrance into and experiencing God's glory is our purpose and destiny – the reason that we were called and chosen by God from the beginning. The question then is, how do we "gain the glory?" Another scripture that speaks of this purpose is Hebrews 2:9-11:

"But we do see Him who has been made for a little while lower than the angels, namely, Jesus, because of the suffering of death crowned with glory and honor, that by the grace of God he might taste death for everyone. For it was fitting for Him, for whom are all things, and through whom are all things, in **bringing many sons to glory**, *to perfect the author of their salvation through sufferings."*

The experience and effect of God's glory manifested in and upon human beings can be clearly demonstrated in scripture also. Take for example, Daniel 8:18, "Now as he [the angel] was speaking with me, I was in a *deep sleep with my face to the ground*, but he touched me, and stood me upright," and Daniel 10:9 "But I heard the sound of his words, (the angel who appears in verses 5 and 6), and as soon as I heard the sound of his words, *I fell into a deep sleep* on my face, with my face to the ground." Also note I Kings 8:10-11, at the celebration of the Feast of Tabernacles (v. 2) when Solomon dedicated the temple and the priests placed the ark of the covenant there: "And it came about that when the priests came from the holy place, that the cloud filled the house of the LORD, so that *the priests could not stand to minister* because of the cloud, for the glory of the LORD filled the house of the LORD."

Zechariah says, in Zechariah 4:1, "Then the angel who was speaking with me returned, and roused me *as a man who is awakened from his sleep.*" Note also, on the Mount of Transfiguration, in Luke 9:32, "Now Peter and his companions *had been overcome with sleep,* but when they were fully awake, they saw His *glory* and the two men standing with Him.:" Note also, Revelation 1:17, John's experience: "And when I saw Him, I fell at His feet *as a dead man.*" Thus, it is clear from these and other passages that effect of the glory is disabling and renders one's entire being completely inert.

So, it is true then, the saying I was first taught by Steve Gray, my friend and mentor who brought this experience with him from his missionary activity in East Africa: "The anointing enables, and the glory *disables.*"

CHAPTER 3
GLORY VS. ANOINTING

You, the reader, may now say to yourself, "So what?" "What's the big deal?" Does differentiating the glory from the anointing really matter, or is it merely "splitting theological hairs?" In reality, the importance of this distinction is *critical* to your spiritual survival as a last-days believer, because without this understanding, you may find yourself caught up in a last-days wave of "strong delusion" (II Thessalonians 2:11) sent (amazingly) by *God Himself* to separate the wheat from the chaff. What could this "strong delusion" be? The Second Epistle of Peter and the Epistle of Jude warn of a plethora of false prophets and teachers who will be active in the Church in the last days.

Perhaps the sternest evidence of this is in Matthew 7:21-23, where Jesus Himself says, "Not everyone who says to Me, 'Lord, Lord' will enter the kingdom of heaven, but he who *does the will of My Father* who is in heaven. Many will say to Me on that day, 'Lord, Lord, did we not *prophesy* in Your name, and in Your name *cast out demons*, and in Your name *perform many miracles*? And then I will declare to them, I never knew you, depart from me, you who practice lawlessness."

Notice that Jesus never says they did these things through the power of Satan. In fact, Jesus made it very clear in Matthew 12:26 "if Satan casts out Satan, he is divided against himself; how then shall his kingdom stand?" So the issue here is not where these people got the power to do these things. Jesus said in Matthew 12:28: "I cast out demons by the Spirit of God." However, the people in this passage that are actually *promoting themselves* in front of Jesus, i.e., "did *we* not prophesy," etc.. They call Him "Lord, Lord," and are performing supernatural works, including casting out demons in His name without His approval as part of an agenda of vainglory and self-aggrandizement which Jesus calls "iniquity," i.e., calling Jesus "Lord" but doing works which are "not the will of My Father who is Heaven."

How could this be, you ask? Consider the Syrophoenician Woman in Matthew 15: 22-28. She was a Gentile, but her persistent, demanding faith prevailed on Jesus, so much so that He cast a demon out of her daughter, despite His statement to her that "I was sent only to the lost sheep of the House of Israel" (Matthew 15.24) and "It is not good to take the children's bread and throw it to the dogs." (Matthew 15:26.) Jesus considered this miracle of deliverance out of bounds and inappropriate, yet the woman got what she wanted because her faith overrode clearly established boundaries set by God Himself. Operating in the realm of faith and getting the Holy Spirit to do miracles for (*and through*) you does not necessarily mean you have God's approval, or that you are one of His sheep. God may just be giving you over to what *you* want (more on this later).

Wherever someone's name appears twice in the New Testament, it is an indication of relationship, i.e., *Simon, Simon* (Luke 22:31), or *Martha, Martha* (Luke 10:41). However, those in Matthew 7:21-23 presume upon a "relationship" with the Lord, but only to harness His power *for themselves* - an anointing by the Holy Spirit to operate in the supernatural. Meanwhile, their *character* is never conformed to the selfless nature of Christ. Addressing this issue in his letter to the Romans, Paul makes a very relevant statement: "if anyone does not have the *Spirit of Christ*, he does not belong to Him." Romans 8:9. Is it possible, then, to have the power and anointing of the Holy Spirit, and not have the Spirit of Christ?

The answer is most emphatically YES– and understanding this distinction is critical for us as believers in this day and age, that is, if we don't want to end up like those unfortunate souls in Matthew 7:21-23. And the way our character is transformed to that of Christ is by "beholding as in a mirror the glory of the Lord." II Corinthians 3:18. Access to the glory will produce this transformation. The anointing of the Holy Spirit may empower us, but there is no scriptural guarantee that it will transform our character. This is because the primary purpose of the Holy Spirit's power and anointing is, according to Acts 1:8, to "be My witnesses" to the lost. Its secondary purpose is succinctly stated in I Corinthians 12:7: "To each is given the manifestation of the Spirit for the common good," i.e., edification, of the Body of Christ. In both cases, the Holy Spirit works *through you* to reach out and touch others, whether it be a lost soul or a fellow member of the Body. The glory, on the other hand, works *on you*, transforming your character from within.

CHAPTER 4
THE HOLY SPIRIT AND THE SPIRIT OF CHRIST

God has promised in the last days to pour out His Holy Spirit on "all flesh" (Acts 2:17). However, just because you may be able to operate in the anointing realm of the Spirit does not necessarily mean you belong to Christ, or that "He ever knew you," in the sense described in Matthew 7:23. Why? Because receiving the Holy Spirit does not mean you have received the Spirit of Christ. They are two different spirits.

How could that be true? Maybe you have assumed, like many Christians, that the Spirit of Christ and the Spirit of God are synonymous, just like many assume the anointing and the glory are synonymous. Neither assumption is true. The spirit of Christ cannot be the same entity as the Holy Spirit. James 2:26 says, "the body without the spirit is dead." When Jesus was baptized at the River Jordan, he was alive by virtue of having a human spirit within Him. He was not dead. Matthew 3:13 says "Then Jesus arrived from Galilee at the Jordan, coming to John, to be baptized by him." Matthew 3:16 says " . . . he saw the Spirit of God descending as a dove, and coming upon Him." The spirit of Christ and the Spirit of God are two different spirits.

Jesus had a human spirit, or his body would have been dead, standing at the Jordan, when the Spirit of God came on Him. His spirit is the sinless human spirit that He gave over to God when, on the cross, he "cried out with a loud voice, and yielded up His spirit." Matthew 27:50. The spirit of Christ, the spirit of sacrifice, the spirit willing to die completely to self, is that spirit that motivated Him to "empty Himself, taking the form of a bond-servant, being made in the likeness of men . . . becoming obedient to the point of death, even death on a cross." Philippians 2:7-8. So it is this spirit within Jesus that Paul is referring to in Romans 8:9 when he says "if any man has not the spirit of

Christ, he does not belong to Him." Paul also emphasized
that "the one who joins himself to the Lord is one spirit
with Him." I Corinthians 6:17.

That sacrificial spirit of Christ, who gave Himself
up for us all, shed His blood, died on the cross and rose
again, is the spirit we need to be one with. The Holy Spirit
does not and cannot save anyone. The Holy Spirit was not
given the job of salvation – that was entrusted to Jesus.
The Holy Spirit did not die for us. Jesus did. We must be
joined to the spirit of Christ, His human spirit, of sacrifice,
of humility, of unconditional love, in order to belong to
Him. We must be willing to be conformed to His image
through the same process of self-denial, of suffering, to
"drink of the cup that I am about to drink." Matthew
20:21. Jesus said "Whoever does not carry his own cross
and come after Me *cannot be My disciple.*" Luke 14:27. So we
see that it is only those who drink of His cup, who carry
their cross, who are truly His disciples.

The reality is "be careful what you ask for, you just
might receive it!" God will give you over to what you really
want. He gave the Israelites quail in the wilderness until it
came out their noses and they became sick of it, (Numbers
11:18-20), and then He sent a plague and destroyed many
of them for craving and demanding it. (Psalms 106:15). In
Judges 8:7-22, He told Samuel to go ahead and give the
nation of Israel their king that they insisted upon, instead
of being ruled over by God Himself. Scripture plainly
states that King Saul was "anointed" by the LORD (I
Samuel 10:1) and the Spirit of the LORD came upon him
mightily and he prophesied (I Samuel 10:6). It even
became a byword among the people, "is Saul also among
the prophets?" But operating in the anointing of the Spirit
and prophesying did not change Saul's character, and he
eventually became an enemy to God's purposes, as
evidenced in the life of David. Saul, who had the anointing
of the Spirit, was persecuting David, who had the
sacrificial and suffering spirit of Christ. Yes, Saul had the
Spirit of God, but *King David had the spirit of Christ.*

How do we know this? Because I Peter 1:11 says
that Old Testament prophets were "seeking to know what
person or time *the Spirit of Christ within them* was indicating
as He (the Spirit of Christ) predicted the sufferings of

Christ and the glories to follow." This means that it was *the spirit of Christ in David* predicting the sufferings of Christ when David penned Psalm 22:16-17: "For dogs have surrounding me, a band of evildoers has encompassed me; *they have pierced my hands and my feet,* I can count all my bones, they look they stare at me, they divide my garments among them, and for my clothing they cast lots." That same spirit of Christ was evident all throughout David's life as he endured persecution, affliction and suffering for the sake of what God called him to be and to do. I believe the Spirit of Christ within David also drove him in his unique desire to establish the Tabernacle of David, the divisions and assignments of the Levitical musicians and singers -- and to bring the Ark of the Covenant (representing the glory) to its rightful resting place in the Holy of Holies in Jerusalem.

      In the same way, there is even now a last-days outpouring of the Spirit, and, in the midst of it, God has *given many over to their desire* to operate in the "anointing," (some are even calling it the Glory), but, like King Saul, their lifestyle and character does not reflect the selfless spirit of Christ. Instead, their bloated, self-serving and carnal lifestyles are a disgrace to the Church, leading many astray and discrediting the true moving of the Spirit. It can truly be said of such people, "all day long the name of God is blasphemed among the Gentiles because of you." (Romans 2:24). That is because the anointing of the Spirit has to do with the *empowerment of self,* and the glory, which conforms us to the image and spirit of Christ, is about *death to self.* How does this conforming process –this inner *character transformatio*n -- happen? Again we must go to II Corinthians 3:18: "but we all, with *unveiled face,* beholding as in a mirror the glory of the Lord, are being *transformed into the same image* from glory to glory." The apostle John said it this way: "when He (Jesus) appears (in Glory), *we shall be like Him,* because we shall see Him just as He is." So how do we "lay hold of the hope set before us . . . a hope both sure and steadfast and one which *enters within the veil.*" (Heb.7:19). How do we remove the veil and behold Him?

How can we gain access to the Glory of God so this transformation process can occur? How do we truly embrace death to self?

CHAPTER 5
TABERNACLE TYPOLOGY AND THE GLORY

Scripture teaches us in I Corinthians 10 that "these things (the events that happened to Israel in the Wilderness) happened to them as an example, and they were written for our instruction, upon whom the ends of the ages have come." This principle is also spoken of in Colossians 2:16-17 (Let no one act as your judge in regard to food or drink or in respect to a Feast day or new moon or Sabbath day – things which are a *mere shadow* (or type) *of what is to come,* but the substance belongs to Christ). Thus, all these Old Testament examples point to another, deeper spiritual reality which is summed up in the person of Jesus Christ. Upon this scriptural principle of typology, we can build an understanding of our own makeup and nature as human beings, and also the makeup and nature of God. We can learn the difference between the anointing and the glory, and how to *enter within the veil.* (Hebrews 7:19).

The first premise we have to start with is from John 2:19-21, "Jesus answered and said to them, "Destroy this temple and in three days I will raise it up. The Jews therefore said, "It took forty-six years to build this temple, and will You raise it up in three days?" But He was speaking of *the temple of His body.*" Paul also confirms this truth in I Corinthians. 3:16 "Do you not know that you are a *temple of God,* and that the Spirit of God dwells in you?" It appears again in I Corinthians 6:19 ("Or do you not know that your body is a *temple of the Holy Spirit* who is in you, whom you have from God, and that you are not your own?") If we are the temple of God, then our makeup consists of and is described by (and symbolized by) the unique design, architecture and articles within the temple of God that were so carefully laid out in Scripture. This carefully detailed set of examples, like the food and drink, Feast days, new moons and Sabbath days mentioned in Colossians 2:16-17, are physical types and shadows pointing us to a spiritual reality of who we are as "the temple of God."

The physical layout of the tabernacle (which was transferred to and became a permanent temple) is described in Exodus 25, 26 and 27 and again in Hebrews 9. These details are important, because they describe *your internal makeup as a human being*. There was a brazen altar of sacrifice where the animals were slain, and a brazen laver (or washbasin) where the priests bathed themselves to purify them for service. These things have to do with the external physical body. Your body has blood, and needs to be cleansed (hopefully daily!) In spiritual terms, these things symbolize the ministry of Jesus, who is God in fleshly form, whom we receive at our initial conversion or salvation experience, through receiving his sacrifice and the shedding of his blood, and the cleansing of the water (water baptism).

The next area (behind a first veil) is called The Holy Place. It contained a seven-pronged candlestick (or lampstand) which is called the Menorah, which was an oil lamp. Also present were a Table of Showbread, where twelve fresh loaves of bread (representing the nation of Israel) were presented to God every day. Also present was a golden Altar of Incense upon which the priest burned incense as an offering to the LORD. In tabernacle typology, these articles are:

Menorah -- the Mind

Showbread – the Will

Incense -- the Emotions

This area is where the priests ministered daily in the Old Testament, and, spiritually speaking, where the Holy Spirit ministers in the New Testament dispensation. The Holy Spirit brings revelation to the mind, reveals God's will and convicts us to yield our will to His as we present our will daily to Him. The incense represents the expression of our emotions which, through the anointing of the Holy Spirit, are released through worship to God. This area of the Holy Place is where the operation of the anointing takes center stage – oil is necessary for the Menorah to give light. This "Holy Place" area is where I would estimate that 99% of the Charismatic church is focused today. This is the place of ministry, of anointing, of worship, operation of spiritual gifts and revelation of God's word, etc. This area is where God ministers to SELF. The mind, emotions and will are the components of your soul – your self-life – the part of you that is conscious of you.

The last area, behind the second veil, is called, "the Holy of Holies." In Old Testament times, it physically contained the Ark of the Covenant, on top of which were two golden cherubim (angels) facing each other, a place called "the Mercy Seat." The Mercy Seat above the Ark is where the Glory of God the Father appeared. This area has to do with the Father. Access to this area in the Old Testament (and access to the Ark before it was placed in the temple) was *extremely* limited and dangerous, because God's glory was deadly to people who came near it or tried to access it without His prior, detailed authorization and prescribed manner for access being followed. The fear of the LORD and possible instant death by God's direct hand were very real in Moses' time and afterwards, up to and including David's time, more than 1000 years later, where "He (God) struck down some of the men of Beth-Shemesh because they looked into the ark of the LORD." I Samuel 6:19. After that, the children of Israel left the Ark alone – for years.

A number of years after the judgment at Beth-Shemesh, Uzzah, one of David's servants was also killed (II Samuel 6:6-7) by the glory of God. Unfortunately, Uzzah tried to steady the Ark as it almost fell off of a cart driven by oxen (not the prescribed mode of transportation). After that, David got mad at God for killing Uzzah and abandoned the Ark for a number of years, afraid to get near it. Years later the Ark was finally placed on the shoulders of priests and carried on poles placed through rings in the sides of it (as God commanded it to be transported in Exodus 25:14) and deposited in the temple of Solomon. After that, the glory of God came out of the Holy of Holies and into the Holy Place as a cloud, *totally incapacitating the priests*. (I Kings 8:10-11). They were *unable to stand to minister*, but thankfully they were not killed, because they had handled the Ark properly and reverently.

CHAPTER 6
MINISTERING IN THE GLORY?

A gain, this passage of scripture calls into serious question the claims of some today that they "minister in the Glory." It certainly didn't happen in Solomon's Temple, and I dare say, at the risk of offending some folks, IT DOESN'T HAPPEN ANYWHERE ELSE, either. It is *physically impossible* to "minister in the Glory." You are either totally unconscious or something very close to it – that is, if it is God's glory we are talking about. At least that is what scripture makes clear, especially in this passage in I Kings 8. The Glory is not about man! Man is totally disabled by it. People minister in the anointing and think that the anointing is the Glory, but it is NOT! Those who have genuinely experienced the Glory know that it is extremely debilitating, and that it is barely possible to even think, let alone move, and most people are rendered unconscious, sometimes for hours at a time. In 1973 I personally witnessed a woman who was picked up 8 feet in the air (while seated in a metal folding chair} and thrown a distance of 25 feet over the top of the congregation to the other side of the building, where she crash landed, chair and all, and lay, totally immobile – for a very long time. She was presumed dead. Who could survive such a thing? (we thought) The congregation was terrified. After a long time (and the administration of smelling salts) she eventually "came to" and was able to sit up and speak. She had been totally healed of diverticulitis. Her testimony of healing was medically confirmed the following week. But she also had an encounter with the Glory of God. He is sovereign. No flesh will share his glory or siphon it off onto themselves.

There are varying degrees of the Glory experience in Scripture and in the experiences of many modern day Christian believers. Isaiah's account in Chapter 6, the angelic visitations of Daniel 8 and 10, the priests at the dedication of Solomon's temple and the disciples' Mount of Transfiguration encounter all describe high-end, extreme and incapacitating experiences of this phenomenon. However, just as Paul described in I Corinthians 15:41 how the glory of the sun differs from the glory of the moon and the stars, so it is with experiences of God's Glory.

Ruth Heflin's book *The Glory* was subtitled *the Atmosphere of Heaven*. Others who have come later, such as David Herzog and Guillermo Maldonado, speak of the Glory as a supernatural atmosphere in which heaven invades earth and miracles seem to occur easily and effortlessly. I believe heaven is filled with God's glory, but the Glory experience that this book is about is more than just the atmosphere of heaven. It is a direct encounter with the divine essence of the Person of God the Father.

Perhaps the best way to understand what the "Glory" actually is would be to liken it to nuclear radiation. One could be around Chernobyl even today, more than 30 years after its nuclear reactor exploded, and, with the proper testing equipment, measure residual atomic radiation which still renders the immediate area harmful to humans and animals. Chernobyl's "atmosphere" of radiation is still present, still affecting all life within a certain geographical area, but not anywhere near the degree of the explosion and the powerful radioactive energy that emanated from the reactor itself. Chernobyl's meltdown is qualitatively and quantitatively different than its residual atmosphere, much in the same way that the experience of a heavenly atmosphere is different from an actual, direct and debilitating radioactive encounter produced by close proximity to a Heavenly Being.

Having said this, claims to be able to "minister in the Glory" I believe are made by sincere people who have experienced the "atmosphere of heaven" and are genuinely anointed by the Holy Spirit for powerful supernatural ministry. However, many seem to be misinformed, promoting themselves, and obviously have not had a direct, "radioactive" encounter with the Father that is totally debilitating. The glory is NOT the anointing. Almighty God takes center stage – He takes OVER – and no one can speak or do anything. The fear of Almighty God can be overwhelming, but more often than not, people are simply rendered totally unconscious, useless and immobile, like the woman catapulted across the room in my previous example was (however God chooses to do it is his prerogative). From Scripture as well as my experience and observation, the Glory seems to be a wonderfully misty, foggy state of delirium resembling deep sleep – a God-induced coma/paralysis as close to physical death as God will allow, without actually killing a person. One might say it is God's "tranquilizer dart" like those used by forestry officials on a wild animal to tag it without its interference or resistance– only He uses the glory on us so he can "tag" us with Jesus' nature – without our interference or resistance.

Thus, we see from temple typology, other parts of scripture, and actual experience, that the Glory of God is in a different area from where the anointing is and has nothing to do with ministry, or the activity of man. Approaching it improperly or irreverently can mean certain death. Its purpose is to conform the believer to Christ's death, and transform that person into someone who is willing to die, even be martyred like Stephen, at a moment's notice. Life on earth is no longer important. Self is GONE!! What used to matter is out the window completely. As Paul put it, "For me to live is Christ and to die is gain."

The Holy of Holies is the "nuclear reactor" where God the Father's glory radiates. That radiation was described by the prophet Ezekiel 1:27-28 where he speaks of a "radiance" in the form of a rainbow (also mentioned by John in Revelation 4:3). It also is described by Habakkuk in chapter 3:4 "His radiance is like the sunlight; He has rays flashing from His Hand." God the Father is called "the God of our Lord Jesus Christ, the Father of Glory" in Ephesians 1:17. God's glory radiates from the face of Christ (II Corinthians 4:6) as it once radiated on earth from Moses' face (Exodus 34:33-35) because of His face to face encounters with the Father. It also radiated from Stephen's face (Acts 6:15) and from the face of the angel who spoke with Daniel in Daniel 10:5. The glory radiated from Jesus' physical body on the Mount of

Transfiguration in Luke 9:29. The glory is spoken of by
Paul as having a "weight" in II Corinthians 4:17. The glory
"has shone in our hearts" (our human spirit), according to
II Corinthians 4:6. That means that the Holy of Holies
corresponds to the spirit of man.

CHAPTER 7
THE GLORY – DEATH AND SUFFERING

In order to get near God's glory, we must be willing to beyond the veil that has "MY LIFE" emblazoned on it. You must be willing to leave your whole life behind. This means going past the anointing oil, the ministry of the Holy Spirit, prophecy, etc. – in other words, everything having to do with things "charismatic" (translate: spiritual self-seeking and self-aggrandizement) – in order to come in contact with the Glory. In a very real sense, you don't come to the Glory. The Glory comes to you – on God's terms, in His time, by His initiative. This is God the Father we are talking about. YAHVEH. The Holy One of Israel who created the universe. Yes, "we have confidence to enter the Holy Place by the blood of Jesus, by a new and living way which He inaugurated for us through the veil, that is, His flesh." (Hebrews 10:19-20). But notice that it says "Holy Place" – not Holy of Holies. We can confidently enter the realm of the Spirit, the operation of the anointing, we can prophesy, lay on of hands, etc. The Glory of the Father -- this is another place altogether. This place is about death to self. Few people want to go there, because it's "not about YOU", i.e., self-empowerment, prosperity, secrets to answered prayer, discovering my destiny, how to be healed, operate in the supernatural, build my church, release my spiritual gifts, etc. This is the place where you cease to exist. For scriptural support, look at Psalms 46:10 - "Be still, and know that I am GOD." I am told the sense of the Hebrew in that passage is really, *cease to exist*, and know that I am God." This gives the expression, "let go and let God" a whole new meaning.

Paul said in II Corinthians 4: 17 that "our *light affliction* is producing a far greater weight of glory." What is the *light affliction* he is talking about? He must be referring to the earlier items in I Corinthians 4:7-10; i.e., "afflicted in every way, but not crushed; perplexed, but not despairing, persecuted, but not forsaken, struck down, but not destroyed, always carrying about in the body the dying of Jesus") – the "dying of Jesus" being "imprisonments, beaten times without number, often in danger of death, five times I received from the Jews thirty nine lashes, three

times I was beaten with rods, once I was stoned, etc." as
explicitly set forth in II Corinthians 11:23-25. Here Paul
clearly connects the weight of glory with affliction – he
calls it *light affliction!* This is NOT for the faint of heart. No
charismatic dabblers, please. This won't be a seeker-
sensitive popular conference topic.

Also notice what the topic of conversation was on
the Mount of Transfiguration in Luke 9:31. Moses and
Elijah "who, appearing in glory, were *speaking of His
departure*, which He (Jesus) was about to accomplish at
Jerusalem." They were discussing His death! How edifying!
These two passages just mentioned are not being
juxtapositioned for effect. Both deal with affliction, with
the "dying of Jesus," as Paul put it. One is about Paul's
cross that he had to carry. The other is literally about the
"dying of Jesus." Both are connected to the glory. What
about Stephen? In Acts 6 and 7 his face shines with the
glory, then He "looked up into heaven and saw the glory
of God." (Acts 7:55). He is stoned to death immediately
afterward. Coincidence? I think not. This is where passages
like Matt 10:39 "He who has found his life shall lose it, and
he who has lost his life for My sake shall find it" start to
come to mind. Luke 9:23-24 begins to resonate: "And He
was saying to them all, "If anyone wishes to come after
Me, *let him deny himself*, and take up his cross daily, and
follow me, for whoever wishes to save his life shall lose it,
but whoever *loses his life* for My sake, he is the one who will
save it."

CHAPTER 8
THE GLORY AND UNITY

In John 17, often referred to as the High Priestly Prayer of Christ, He is praying "I do not pray for these alone, but also for those who will believe in Me through their word, that they may be one, as You, Father, are in Me and I in You, that the world may believe that you sent me, and the *glory which you gave me, I have given them*, that they may be one, even as we are one, I in them, and You in me, that they made be made perfect in one, and that the world may know that You have sent Me, and have love them as You have loved Me. Father, I desire that they also whom You gave Me may be with Me where I am, *that they may behold My glory* which You have given Me, for You loved me before the foundation of the world." John 17:20-26.

Jesus' prayer for oneness is often spoken of as the one prayer of His on earth that God has not answered yet. I believe the reason for this is tied to the Church's experience (or lack thereof) of the glory, and entry into it by the total embracing of death to self that Jesus entire life (and death) exemplified. The experience of the glory will bring true oneness among believers – oneness with the Spirit of Christ, the Holy Spirit and God the Father. The fruit of the glory experience is the desire to be one with the LORD and to die to all that is not of Him.

The Glory is what makes the Trinity three persons *but only one will*. Only the glory – beholding Jesus' glory which God has given Him – will make believers like the Trinity is -- one heart and mind (and will) -- and melt away the fleshly and religious divisions and vain traditions that have separated Christians to the present day. The anointing cannot accomplish this and was not designed to do so. The primary purpose of the anointing and empowering of the Spirit was to make believers effective witnesses to the lost, as Jesus stated in Acts 1:8 "But you shall receive power when the Holy Spirit has come upon you, and you shall be witnesses to Me in Jerusalem, and in all Judea, and Samaria, and to the end of the earth."

The Church has received power. The Holy Spirit has come. Particularly since the Azusa Street revival in 1906, the power of the Holy Spirit has truly swept across "to the end of the earth." But when the glory Jesus shares with God the Father comes upon and takes over a person, a congregation, a Church – that Church will manifest the loving, self-sacrificing giving nature of the Father, who "so loved the world, that He gave His only begotten Son." John 3:16. It is time for the Church to "behold Jesus' glory, which God has given Him" John 17:24, so that the Church may truly become the Bride of Christ, prepared for His return -- that she may become unified within herself and one with her Bridegroom.

CHAPTER 9
THE GLORY AND DESTINY
ACCELERATION

When I first heard of the man who became my dear friend and mentor, evangelist and missionary Stephen Gray, he was sending e-mail reports in 1999 and 2000 of entire villages in Muslim areas of east Africa experiencing the Glory of God at a meeting. Steve would announce an evangelistic or gospel meeting, and those who came, after hearing a simple message of repentance and surrender to Christ, were suddenly overwhelmed all at once with such a powerful weight of God's glory that the entire congregation was struck down, some wailing in fear, most totally immobilized, for long periods of time. One is reminded of Psalms 119:120: "My flesh trembles for fear of Thee, and I am afraid of Thy judgments." Steve Gray captured this phenomenon on video while it was happening in a meeting in coastal Tanzania near the city of Dar-es-Salaam. To see an entire congregation of African Muslims struck down to the floor, some trembling, others shrieking and wailing, many unconscious -- is absolutely unnerving yet electrifying to watch – not a typical church service!

After that experience, these former Muslims were so radically transformed by this encounter that they were literally willing to die for Jesus. In reality, they knew that for them, the cost of becoming a Christian meant they faced the imminent threat *of certain death* from a member of their family by converting from Islam to another religion. I believe that was why the Glory of God was so powerfully manifested among these people in these meetings – because turning to Christ for them literally meant *dying – and they were ready to do it*. Not only were they ready to die for Jesus, but they were eager to live for Him, too, radically committed with all their might. What was most notable was the astonishing spiritual maturity they demonstrated in a very short time.

Steve Gray, in his repeated experiences of this phenomenon in Africa, compared it to the difference between merely watering a plant and feeding it Miracle Grow! Yet there was a logical and definable reason why this sudden transformation and seemingly instantaneous maturity level was manifested. This aspect of God's glory has become very apparent to me ever since I began to first take notice of it in 2003. The reality is that the Glory of God is *radiation* -- similar to particle acceleration in a nuclear reactor in the natural realm. We know that radiation in the natural realm has the ability to accelerate the mutation of DNA and permanently alter (and damage) cell structure. Amazingly, the same is true in the spirit realm. The Glory of God – the radiation of His core energy – His divine attributes of love, wisdom, majesty, excellence, faithfulness, integrity, etc. -- will accelerate mutation of the character of the person undergoing the radiation.

This "particle acceleration" process is described in Exodus 33:18-19 and Exodus 34:7-8. Moses asks God to reveal His glory. The LORD passes by in front of Moses and proclaims his nature and character: "the LORD, the LORD God, compassionate, and gracious, slow to anger and abounding in lovingkindness and truth, who keeps lovingkindness for thousands, who forgives iniquity, transgression and sin." Exodus 34:7,8. When God radiates His Glory, what happens next is that the ultimate identity that the person exposed to it was created and destined to be – all the fully matured character traits God has foreknown from eternity – suddenly are accelerated and come into full fruition of being in the here and now. The effect is like a plant bursting through the ground and growing to full flowering and fruit bearing in an instant, as can be depicted by fast motion photography. Unfortunately, this is true whether the person's ultimate spiritual destiny and inner character is good or evil, heavenly or hell-bound. This reality can be shown time and time again in Scripture.

Where is this in the Bible? One very clear example is in Exodus 24:16-18 as it relates to Exodus 32. The children of Israel were in the presence of God's glory for forty days at Mount Sinai while He communed with Moses and transmitted the Torah to him on the mountain. What happened to the nation of Israel during that time?

Amazingly, all the inner character, the ultimate nature and destiny of who they were to become, suddenly sprang forth in Exodus 32. They immediately went into idolatry, rebelled against God and Moses, they built a golden calf, and became what God describes them as in Exodus 32 ("Thy people have corrupted themselves.") Although we think of "corruption" as a gradual process of decay, the children of Israel were accelerated into corruption very quickly by their exposure to the Glory emanating from Mount Sinai. What they ultimately became is also graphically laid out in Psalm 106. You would think that Israel would have been in awe of God and worshipping Him as the whole nation witnessed His Glory of God at the same time on Sinai. Instead, they quickly were propelled into their ultimate spiritual character and destiny – a rebellious, idolatrous, evil generation whose bleached bones littered the wilderness, never entering the Promised Land. Even Moses is not immune. His continual exposure to the Glory (Exodus 34:35 "the skin of Moses' face shone") brings his anger management problem to the surface as described in Numbers 27:16, 17 where the LORD tells Moses his volcanic display of anger and frustration at the waters of Meribah – even after years of being in God's glory – are going to also disqualify him from entering the Promised Land, just as the people he led were excluded.

In the same manner, King David also (at first) exhibits godly character and performs great exploits, beginning with his victory over Goliath right up until shortly after his encounter with the ark of God, (i.e., where His Glory was deposited, contained, and radiated from – a portable nuclear reactor, if you like.) Notice in II Samuel 6:5-10, when, while David is celebrating the bringing of the ark to Jerusalem, he suddenly becomes angry, offended and afraid of the LORD after His glory breaks forth upon David's servant Uzzah, killing him. As a result, David abandons the ark right there for three months. By II Samuel 11, he has quit going into battle with his army, and then, while the army is away fighting the Philistines, David falls into adultery and murder over Bathsheba. After his exposure to the glory, all the ugliness and nastiness of what was in David's sinful character starts rising to the surface and ultimately bears fruit. We see this also in the lives of the disciples of Jesus, who, at the Passover meal in John 17, are with Jesus as He prays "glorify Thy Son" and says "the glory that Thou has given Me I have given them." However, right after these statements, "all the disciples forsook Him and fled" Matthew 26:56. Peter then curses and swears that he does not know Jesus in Matthew 26:74 and Judas' ultimate destiny as the "son of perdition" is fulfilled.

Another example is in Acts – the martyrdom of Stephen. Notice the Sanhedrin, "saw Stephen's face like the face of an angel" (Acts 6:15) and while Stephen "gazed intently into heaven and saw the Glory of God" the Sanhedrin "cried out with a loud voice and covered their ears, and they rushed upon him with one impulse." Acts 7:55-57. The Sanhedrin's ultimate character and destiny accelerates into full blown, intense murderous hatred of Stephen, and everything the Church stood for, as Stephen manifests and radiates the Glory. In fact, their persecution of the whole church "arose that very day in Jerusalem," affecting the whole church as it existed at that time (Acts 8:1-4). Saul of Tarsus, a participant in Stephen's stoning, (Acts 22:20), is catapulted into a ruthless, aggressive campaign of "breathing threats and murder against the disciples" (Acts 7:1). It is only another powerful encounter (Acts 9:1-8) with the Glory – one that knocks Saul to the ground and renders him totally blind – that shifts his destiny from being "the chiefest of sinners" (I Timothy 1:15) to being perhaps the greatest and most effective apostle of them all.

Another interesting and telling example of destiny acceleration after exposure to the Glory is in the life of Michal, the daughter of King Saul. Her father gave her to David as a wife. In I Samuel 18:20 it states that "Michal, Saul's daughter, *loved David*." Saul later became jealous of David, so Saul took Michal away from David and gave her to Palti, from the city of Gallim, after David went on the run to hide from Saul. I Samuel 25:44. Later, upon Saul's death, however, David demanded that Michal be returned to him, and they were reunited. II Samuel 3:13-16. However, when the ark of the LORD, which contained God's glory, "came into the city of David, "Michal the daughter of Saul looked out of the window and saw King David leaping and dancing before the LORD, and she *despised him in her heart*."

II Samuel 6:16. Then she immediately spewed out her venomous contempt and accused David of being some sort of foolish exhibitionist, *just as he is coming home to bless her* and all his household (II Samuel 16:20). She becomes barren and has no child to the day of her death. I Samuel 6:23.

Michal's destiny was accelerated into full flower by the appearance of the ark and the worship of King David as he danced before it. What happened to all the love she once had for him? The glory brought forth and accelerated into being Michal's true character and attitude toward David, and her destiny of being rejected and barren. I believe this is a picture of what is going to happen in the last-days Church, as the "tares" who profess to love Jesus, once they are exposed to the glory, begin to pour out their hatred and contempt upon truly anointed people who only want to bless them. Those who say, "Lord, Lord" are in the same boat as Michal – they may have loved God or Jesus in the beginning, but the Glory will reveal their ultimate destiny and character – bad trees that end up producing bad fruit – devoid of the sacrificial Spirit of Christ.

The Apostle Peter makes this observation in I Peter 4:14: "If you are reviled for the name of Christ, you are blessed, because the Spirit of Glory and of God rests on you." In other words, if the Glory is emanating from you, it will accelerate some people around you into their awful, ungodly ultimate destiny – they will turn on you like Michal turned on David -- and vehemently hate you (*especially* people in the church!) This is because the fully developed nature in them as false believers (see I Corinthians 5:9-11; I Corinthians 16:17-18; II Corinthians 11:26) ends up hating Jesus and His followers. I have unfortunately experienced this phenomenon of unexplainable, vicious hatred, out of nowhere, most of it, unfortunately from so-called "Spirit-filled Christians" -- for no apparent reason, and in great intensity -- since I encountered the Glory in 2003 and it began to rest on me. If you, the Reader, enter this experience of the Glory, you can be certain that other people in church that formerly loved you will suddenly turn on you and hate you. Do not be surprised when this occurs, because it is the acceleration of their destiny.

In reference to the Glory and destiny/character acceleration, I must also mention a phenomenon known as the "Jerusalem Syndrome." Before my first trip to Israel in

2003, my wife warned me about this "Jerusalem Syndrome." This syndrome is well known among Christian pilgrims who frequent the Holy Land. In a nutshell, what my wife warned me about was that when a typical churchgoing Christian – even *and especially* a pastor – travels to Israel, every undealt with character issue hidden in their life comes boiling up to the surface and gets exposed – usually publicly – in a very ugly and degrading way. Things in their life that they have been able to successfully keep hidden are "shouted from the housetops."

I witnessed this phenomenon first hand when my wife and I organized a number of what are called "Familiarization Tours," special half-price Pastor's Tours offered by the Israeli government as an incentive to ordained ministers to familiarize them with what a typical tour of Israel is like, in the hopes that they will bring their congregation the following year or at some time in the future. Every time my wife put together a Pastor's Tour, she would hold a special orientation meeting and warn the pastors and their wives ahead of time, saying, "Before you go on this trip, make sure you get before the Lord and get your life right, and get repentant before God. Deal with every issue you can possibly address before we go, because you can be sure that if you don't, *it will all come out in front of everyone when we get there!*" During these Pastor's Tours we witnessed the some of the most unimaginable, ugly and intensely selfish, boorish behavior on the part of "Spirit-filled" pastors that we have ever seen, even worse than unbelievers. Much of it was complaints about everything imaginable, total lack of cooperation with (and public, humiliating criticism of) the tour guide, outbursts of totally inappropriate anger, and heated arguments over money. The last Israeli guide we used for our last tour was considered one of the top 3 guides in Israel by the tourism industry. He informed my wife, however, that "our group was the worst behaved group he had ever been on tour within 30 years." We received news of his death shortly after we got home. The saddest part about all this is that our guide was an unsaved, secular Jew, and his last impression of Christians did not make him want to become one.

What does the Jerusalem Syndrome have to do with the Glory? *Everything!* God's Holy Land, and especially Jerusalem, is permeated with the glory. Ruth Ward Heflin knew this, and that's why Ruth Ward Heflin chose to move there and live there, holding her glory meetings and writing her famous book about the Glory. The Glory quickly exposes and brings to the glaring light every hidden, latent character flaw we have. You become who you really are (and always were) when you are in Israel, and you cannot possibly hide it. The same thing happens after a believer is exposed to the glory of God. The wheat and the chaff become painfully obvious to the most casual observer.

The Glory stirs up intense love and intimacy with God and His people for those whose destiny is heaven – and it stirs up ugliness, ungodliness and malicious hatred in those who are "tares," i.e., the imposters in the Church to whom Jesus will someday say, "I never knew you." This process of destiny acceleration is best described by the angel in Revelation 22:11: "Let the one who does wrong, *still do wrong*, and let the one who is filthy, *still be filthy*, and let the one who is righteous, *still practice righteousness*, and let the one who is holy, *still keep himself holy.*" I have been informed that the verbs in the original Greek here are *present progressive*, meaning, more accurately, " let him who is filthy *progressively become even more filthy*," etc. The angel in Revelation 22 is perfectly and accurately describing this process of destiny acceleration coming to the Church as God's glory begins to appear. In Matthew 13:37-43, Jesus speaks of a time at the end of the age when the wheat and the tares will come to full fruition. "As for the good seed, these are the sons of the kingdom; and the tares are the sons of the evil one." This is speaking of two different natures, two different ultimate destinies that the glory of God will accelerate into culmination at the end of this age, which many believe will be in this generation.

The true outpouring of God's glory that is coming will incapacitate entire congregations flat on their faces, inert, awestruck (if not unconscious), and unable to move or utter a sound. I have been fortunate enough to be in meetings like this over the last 10 years and I have witnessed this with my own eyes. In one such meeting, the stillness and silence was so heavy with Glory that the pastor of the church, who was sitting near me, could scarcely breathe the words, "I had a message. *I dare not give it. I dare not quench this.*"

My experience is that unfortunately such meetings are extremely rare. They have been few and far between, primarily because most churches, especially here in America, simply will not let God have His way, no matter how much they sing about it. However, when God's glory suddenly and sovereignly invades His church, man will not be able to prance about in his pomp, flaunting his "anointing." All fleshly entertainment, man-centered wisdom, ingenious and trendy self-promotion programs and other dead works will perish from center stage and God the Father alone will be the center of attention. "The proud look of man will be abased, and the loftiness of man will be humbled, and the LORD alone will be exalted in that day." Isaiah 2:11. He will then expose and accelerate into being, with startling swiftness, the full-blown identity of the Bride and the Harlot, the Wheat and the Tare, as we anxiously look upward for Jesus' soon return. Hosts of angels will descend and uproot the tares, removing *out of His kingdom* "all stumbling blocks and all that offend." Matthew 13:40-41. Then the ultimate destiny of the Bride will be revealed as it is described in Matthew 13:43, quoting from Daniel 12:3: "The righteous will shine forth as the sun in the kingdom of their Father. He who has ears, let him hear."

CHAPTER 10
THE GLORY'S END TIME PURPOSE PREPARING THE BRIDE OF CHRIST

In Ephesians 5:27, Paul gives us the attributes of the Bride of Christ, "that He might to present to Himself the church *in all her glory, having no spot or wrinkle or any such thing, but that she should be holy and blameless.*" In Revelation 19:7-8, John writes: "Let us rejoice and be glad, and give the glory to Him, for the marriage of the Lamb has come, and His bride has *made herself ready. It was given to her to clothe herself in fine linen, bright and clean, for the linen is the righteous acts of the saints.*"

The prevailing question in the minds of many in the Body of Christ is, "how in the world are we going to be without spot, wrinkle or blemish, clothed in bright and clean linen? How are we going to ever make ourselves ready?" It goes without saying that the hour is late, and given all the obvious signs around us, the Lord's coming is soon. No one should have any illusions about the current state of the church, especially in America. Apparently God must do a quick and sovereign work of radical transformation, if these scriptures are ever to be fulfilled. Romans 9:28 says "He will finish the work, and cut it short in righteousness: because *a short work* will the Lord make upon the earth." How will this happen? The answer is found in II Corinthians 3:18: "But we, with *unveiled* face, beholding the *glory of the Lord,* are being transformed into His likeness, from glory to glory, just as from the Lord, the Spirit." The true identity and ultimate destiny of the Bride is *unveiled* in the experience of the glory, which administers radiation treatments to remove the cancer of self-absorbed drama, habitual sin and blatant worldliness and render her clean, spotless and radiant.

As the church rejoices in the hope of this glorious transformation, the church must also keep in mind that destiny acceleration works both positively and negatively, as described in Revelation 22:11. At the same time the Bride is being prepared, being *accelerated into her destiny,* so also is "Bridezilla," the Harlot. Both the wheat and the tares are accelerating and growing into full maturity around one another, as illustrated by Jesus' parable in Matthew 13.

One aspect of the Glory that deserves mention at this point involves the scriptural paradigm of Mary and Martha. In Luke 10:38-42, we see how, after Jesus entered the home of Mary and Martha, Martha was focused on and occupied with much serving, while Mary was seated at Jesus' feet, listening to His words. Martha was indignant with Mary's quiet waiting upon Jesus while she did "all the work." She wanted Jesus' attention focused onto her and her needs, while Mary placed all her attention on Jesus Himself. This story contains within it a larger picture, an end-time parable, if you will, of Mary and Martha within the Church today. My wife and I have seen this parable played out in our experience in different settings over and over again.

Over the past 13 years my wife and I have been having what we call "glory meetings" in our home. Our intent was to have an intimate gathering where we could share what we are learning about the Glory and then, through praise and worship, lead others into a deeply intimate yet corporate encounter with the Glory. What we found, however, was that when we, like Mary, sought to enter into a protracted time of sitting in reverent stillness, waiting upon the Lord, focusing only on His presence – Martha's presence would invariably rear its ugly head. I recall several times where one individual would literally get up on their feet and pace up and down, champing at the bit to prophesy, read a scripture, or otherwise "minister." They could not stand the silence, the stillness – the inactivity. It is because Marthas cannot and will not let go of their overwhelming need to operate in the anointing, to "minister," to pray or read a scripture . . . to in some way divert attention away from the Lord and onto themselves. They simply were not able to leave the Holy Place, where the Holy Spirit's anointing operates and ministers through them (or to them)– and enter into the Holy of Holies, where self is dead and we must "be still and know that I am God." Psalms 46:10. That is where we, "with unveiled face, behold the Glory of the Lord and are changed into His image from

one degree of glory to another." II Corinthians 3:18. Even on the
Mount of Transfiguration, the wonderful "glory meeting"
described in Luke 9, Martha reared her ugly head as Simon Peter
interrupted the Glory encounter to offer his opinion of what was
going on, i.e.,
"Master, it is good for us to be here," and to suggest that they
build three tabernacles – one for Jesus, one for Moses, and one for
Elijah." However, God the Father was in charge of the meeting –
His glory cloud overtook them all, and they heard Him proclaim,
"this is My Beloved Son. Listen to Him" (i.e., it's not about you,
Peter).
At some point, the Bride of Christ must come into the presence of
the Glory and silently behold Him. She will be transformed into
His image, where Jesus can at say, like Adam, "At last! This is bone
of My bone, and flesh of my flesh!" Genesis 2:23. Meanwhile,
Bridezilla, the Harlot, will be busy promoting herself in ministry
and building projects (let us build three tabernacles, etc.).

CHAPTER 11
THE GLORY, THE FATHER
AND ISRAEL'S PRE-EMINENCE

J esus made a very interesting statement in
Matthew11:27: "All things have been
handed over to Me by My Father, and no
one knows the Son, except the Father, nor does
anyone know the Father, except the Son, anyone
to whom the Son wills to reveal Him." He made
another similarly interesting statement in John
14:6: I am the way, the truth and the life; no one
comes to *the Father* but through Me." – (not "no
one gets to heaven when they die except through
me," as is often preached). Although the latter
statement may be true by default, that was not
actually what Jesus was saying here – He was
talking about *access to the Father.* Both these
statements show that it is Jesus' will (and our
destiny as believers) to be brought into a
relationship not only with Jesus, but with the
Father.

In John 14:23, Jesus also says "If anyone
loves Me, he will keep My word, and *My Father will
love him*, and *We will come* to him, and make our
abode with him." Jesus went on to say, "this is
eternal life, that they may *know Thee, the only true
God*, and Jesus Christ whom Thou has sent." John
17:3. Jesus said the Pharisees "receive glory from
one another, but *do not seek the glory that is from the
one and only God.*" John 5:44. He was talking about
His Father, and by inference in this passage,
exhorts us to seek the glory that emanates *only from
Him.*

In his first epistle, the Apostle Peter
makes reference to his personal encounter with

the Father on the mountain of transfiguration, mentioned in Matthew 17, Mark 9 and Luke 9. Peter says, in II Peter 1:16-18: "We did not follow cleverly devised tales when we made known to you the power and coming of our Lord Jesus Christ, but we were *eyewitnesses of His majesty*, for when He received honor and *glory from God the Father*, such an utterance as this was made to Him by the *Majestic Glory*, This is My beloved Son, with whom I am well-pleased, and we ourselves heard this utterance made from heaven when we were with Him on the holy mountain." The reason for emphasizing the Father here is that He is the Majestic Glory. He is the one who reveals Himself throughout Scripture in His glory, and so in order to access "the glory" – *we must access the Father.*

As the book of Hebrews, especially chapter 6 exhorts us, "let us press on to maturity (v. 1) and enter and find refuge "behind the veil, where Jesus has entered as a forerunner for us, having become a High Priest forever according to the order of Melchizedek." (v. 19-20.). For the Church to enter full maturity, it must become what its Forerunner, Jesus became and do what its Forerunner did – enter into and be transfigured by the Majestic Glory of the Father. In so doing, we will be in communion with the Person whom Jesus identified as "the God of Abraham, of Isaac, and of Jacob." Matthew 22.32. He is the God of Israel. Consequently, we cannot hope to embrace Him and be one with Him without embracing what He values very intensely and is so vehemently passionate about – His covenant people Israel, and His beloved city, Jerusalem. Notice that Jesus harshly rebuked the cities of Chorazin, Bethsaida and Capernaum in Galilee for their failure to repent, (Matthew 11:21-24), but he actually broke down and wept over Jerusalem (Luke 19:41). If you want to really understand God's passionate attitude about Jerusalem, then take note of Zechariah 1:14 "I am exceedingly jealous for Jerusalem and Zion." This is repeated in Zechariah 8:1-2; "Then the word of the LORD of hosts came saying, Thus says the LORD of hosts, I am exceedingly jealous for Zion, yes, with great wrath I am jealous for her." Are you? Can you identify with God's attitude about Jerusalem? One cannot hope to be intimate with someone, and yet continue to ignore and be absolutely clueless about the very things they are most passionate about, as much of the Christian church seems to be today.

Jesus said to the Samaritan woman at the well of Sychar: "You worship that which you do not know; we worship that which we know, for *salvation is from the Jews.*" John 4:22. Notice also Paul's passionate attitude towards Israel and the Jewish people, graphically expressed in Romans 9:2-5 "I have *great sorrow and unceasing grief in my heart,* for I could *wish that I myself were accursed, separated from Christ,* for the sake of my brethren, my kinsmen according to the flesh, who are Israelites, to whom belongs the adoption as sons, *and the Glory,* and the covenants, and the giving of the Law, and the temple service, and the promises, whose are the fathers, and from whom is the Christ, according to the flesh, who is over all, God blessed forever." Twice in scripture Paul exhorts us to follow his example, urging, "Be imitators of me, as I am of Christ." I Corinthians 4:16; I Corinthians 11:1. Are we imitators of Paul in this area? Would we ever entertain the thought of giving up our own salvation for the sake of Israel? Do we zealously love Israel and Jerusalem as God does – as Paul does?

According to Romans 9:4, access to the Glory of God is a birthright of the Jewish people. Until the Church repents of its patronizing, disrespectful, arrogant attitude towards the Jews and Israel, and begins to imitate Paul in this area, we cannot reasonably expect to have access to the Father, the Holy One of Israel, and His Glory. As Paul exhorts in Romans 11:17 "But if some of the branches were broken off, and you, being a wild olive, were grafted in among them and became partaker with them of the *rich root of the olive tree*, do not be arrogant toward the branches, but if you are arrogant, remember that it is not you who supports the root, but the root supports you." The key to positioning oneself for an encounter with the Glory is to begin to acknowledge your ignorance of God the Father and His ways, His preferences, His personality -- His value system. The heart – the ROOT-- of His value system is Israel. As Paul says in Romans 11:28-29, "From the standpoint of the gospel they are enemies for your sake, but from the standpoint of God's choice, they are beloved for the sake of the fathers, for *the gifts and the calling of God are irrevocable.*

      Jesus came to reconcile us to the Father. The Holy Spirit is not the be-all and end-all, or the ultimate goal of Christian experience, despite what many charismatic and Pentecostal believers persist in believing. Jesus wants to reveal *the Father* to us -- and at the epicenter of the Father's heart is Israel. In fact, although this may come as a shock to many Christians, *God calls Israel His son, and Jesus, who is the Son, considers Himself to be inseparable in His being from Israel!* WHAT! Where is this in the Bible? What about Exodus 4:22-23, as God tells Moses, "Thus you shall say to Pharaoh, Thus says the LORD, *Israel is my son*, my first-born, so I say to you, let My son go, that he may serve Me, but if you have refused to let him go, behold I will kill your son, your first-born." Consider Jeremiah 31:9 "I am a Father to Israel, and Ephraim is my firstborn;" or Hos. 11:1 "When Israel was a child I loved him, and *out of Egypt I called My son.*" This passage refers to both Israel and Jesus as the son of God, since it is also quoted in Matthew 2:15 as referring to Jesus. What about elsewhere in the New Testament? In Matthew 26:31-40, Jesus is separating *nations* (not individuals) from one another to judge them, saying "Truly I say to you, to the extent that you did it to one of these brothers of Mine, you did it to ME." Simply put, the nation of Israel are his brethren, so much so that what you do to them, you do to Him -- and the other nations are being judged by the way they treated Israel.

How do we know that this is the correct interpretation? Because the Bible says exactly the same thing in Joel 3:2: God's intention, at the end of time, is to *gather all the nations, and enter into judgment with them on behalf of My people and My inheritance, Israel, whom they have scattered among the nations, and they have divided up My land.*" In Zechariah 12:3, the Father says, "And it will come about in that day that I will make Jerusalem a heavy stone for all the peoples, all who lift it will be severely injured. And *all the nations of the earth will be gathered against it.*" The Nation of Israel, in the last days, is going to be the plumb line separating those who know Jesus and those who do not. Is America a "Christian nation?" Then why are we even now trying to shove a "Road Map to Peace" down Israel's throat, dividing up God's land and parcel pieces of it out, pressuring Israel to accept "pre-1967 borders!" God is surely going to judge all nations (including America) for this. This is exactly what Joel 3:2 and Zech. 12:3 are talking about. God is always making a distinction among the nations as to who favors Israel and who doesn't. Ultimately, He will gather all the nations and deal with them about their treatment of Israel, because "He who touches you (Israel) touches the apple of My eye." Zech. 2:8. What you do to Israel, you do to Jesus – and God will orchestrate the battle of Armageddon to judge the nations *specifically for their treatment of Israel.*

Further evidence of Jesus' inseparability from Israel as God's Son is found where Jesus speaks to Saul of Tarsus in Acts 9: "Saul, Saul, why are you persecuting Me?" Jesus is speaking of Himself *as Israel* – his brethren who had received Him as Messiah. But wait a minute -- doesn't this passage refer to the Church, i.e., all believers, including Gentiles? *Absolutely not, because the Gentile "Church" as we know it did not even exist yet!* Peter had not yet visited the household of Cornelius. Saul of Tarsus was still persecuting Jewish believers, attempting, in his mind, to keep the Jewish nation pure and prevent it from being led astray by this heretical new sect which both Saul and the chief priests were determined to stamp out. In so doing, Saul was persecuting the Son of God.

Actually, and this may also seem a shock to many Christians, especially in America -- *the Bible is Israel-centric.* The vast majority of the prophecies of the Bible revolve around Israel - not some metaphoric notion of God's people, but an actual, literal plot of ground in the Middle East, and an actual people group called Jews. Yes, the Father desires that no one perish, and he loves all the nations. But in order to really know God and have His favor (and His Glory) upon your life, you have to acknowledge the pre-eminence He gives Israel and the Jewish people. It is literally true that, in keeping with Paul's olive tree metaphor, Israel remains to this day God's "firstborn son" -- the root of everything that comes to us spiritually as the Church. Paul said it this way in Ephesians 2:18 "Through Him

(Christ), we both (Jews and Gentiles) have our access in one Spirit *to the Father."*

All the major modern outpourings of the Holy Spirit upon the Church (i.e., the Welsh Revival in 1904; Azusa Street Revival in 1906) directly coincide historically with the Zionist movement - the effort to re-establish a Jewish state in the Holy Land. At the end of the nineteenth century and at the beginning of the twentieth, a committed group of Jewish leaders united and organized themselves around this common purpose. As a result, the World Zionist Organization (Hebrew: ההסתדרות הציונית העולמית *HaHistadrut HaTsionit HaOlamit*), or WZO, was founded in 1897 at the First Zionist Congress, held from August 29 to August 31, 1897 in Basle, Switzerland.[1] At that time, Theodore Herzl, David Ben Gurion and others formulated plans for the restoration of a Jewish state in what was then the British controlled territory of "Palestine" with a restored Hebrew language as the official spoken language of the Jews.[2] Interestingly, around the same time in 1896, three Tennessee evangelists (William Martin, Joe M. Tipton, and Milton McNabb) with links to Benjamin H. Irwin's Fire-Baptized Holiness Church, brought the message of entire sanctification to the western North Carolina countryside when they held a revival in the Schearer Schoolhouse near Camp Creek in Cherokee County.[3] A feature of this revival was that some participants, including children, spoke in tongues when they experienced sanctification, thus launching the beginning of the Pentecostal church in America.

Meanwhile in Europe, Jewish emigration to Palestine began in earnest at the turn of the twentieth century.[4] In fact, throughout the entire twentieth century, spectacular periods of revival and explosive growth in the Church have directly paralleled high points in Israel's formation and continued restoration. Obvious examples are the Healing Revival spearheaded by Oral Roberts, Jack Coe, William Branham and others beginning in 1948, the same year Israel became a nation. [5] In 1967, while Israel regained control of Jerusalem in the Six Day War (for the first time in 2,000 years), a charismatic revival broke out in the Roman Catholic Church at Duquesne University, spreading rapidly to all the mainline denominations in what came to be known as the "charismatic renewal." [6] In 1973 as Israel defeated her enemies in the Yom Kippur War, Christian TV was birthed.[7] In 1994, as Israel successfully negotiated the Oslo Peace Accords, tremendous revival broke out at the Toronto Airport Vineyard Church[8] and spread to the Brownsville Revival in Pensacola, Florida the following year,[9] impacting millions and changing the landscape of Christianity for a new generation.[10]

In short, a literal explosion of Christianity has happened across the world since the restoration of Israel began. One amazing example is China, where over 100 million people have come to the Lord (not just nominally, but with radical, miraculous, dynamic testimonies) since 1949 (a year after Israel's birth as a nation). Dramatic prophecies of Israel's return to her land in the latter days are being fulfilled, a theme known as *aliyah (GOING UP)*, found throughout the Old Testament prophets from Moses onward (Deuteronomy 30:4,5). As stated in Jeremiah 30:3 "For behold, the days are coming, says the LORD, that I will bring back from captivity My people Israel and Judah, says the LORD; and I will cause them to return to the land that I gave to their fathers, and they shall possess it." More importantly, countless numbers of Jews are beginning to come to faith in Yeshua (Jesus) as their Messiah, and the number of so-called "Messianic" congregations in Israel is exploding, as more and more young people in Israel become exposed to the Good News and see the signs and wonders that are proliferating among believers. As Israel comes to faith, Paul said (Romans 11:15) it would mean nothing less than "life from the dead." Habakkuk prophesied (Habakkuk 2:14) "For the earth will be filled with the knowledge of the glory of the LORD, as the waters cover the sea." I believe the coming outpouring of the Father's glory is directly tied to mass conversions of Jewish people worldwide, and especially in the Holy Land.

---

[1] Dr. Motti Friedman, The Pedagogic Center, The Department for Jewish Zionist Education, The Jewish Agency for Israel, (c) 1997, 1998, 1999, 2000, *Jewish Virtual Library* – World Zionist Congress, http://www.jewishvirtuallibrary.org/first-to-twelfth-zionist-congress-1897-1921. Accessed June 2011.

[2] Paul Johnson, *A History of the Jews*, New York, New York, Harper Collins, 1987, p.442.

[3] Charles W. Conn, *Like A Mighty Army*, Cleveland, Tennessee, Pathway Press ,1994.

[4] Eran Kaplan, Derek J. Penslar, *The Origins of Israel 1882-1948, A Documentary History*, Madison, WI, University of Wisconsin Press, 2011

[5] D. E. Harrell, *All Things Are Possible: The Healing and Charismatic Revivals in Modern America*, Bloomington, IN, Indiana University Press, 1978 p. 25

[6] Rene Laurentin, *Catholic Pentecostalism*, New York, New York: Doubleday & Company. 1977, pp. 23–24.

[7] Mark Ward Sr., *The Electronic Church in the Digital Age: Cultural Impacts of Evangelical Mass Media [2 volumes]: Cultural Impacts of Evangelical Mass Media*, ABC-CLIO, USA, 2015, page 206

[8] Vinson Synan, *The Holiness-Pentecostal Tradition*, Grand Rapids, MI, Eerdmans Publishing Co., 1997.

---

[9] Alice Crann, *"Pastor orchestrated first revival"*. The Pensacola News Journal. November 19, 1997.

[10] Steve Rabey. "Fire From Above". *Charisma Magazine*. Lake Mary, Florida, June 2005

CHAPTER 12
THE GLORY AND SHABBAT
GOD'S SABBATH REST

Hebrews 4:1 states, "Therefore, let us fear lest, while a promise remains of entering His rest, any of you should seem to have come short of it." Later in the chapter it is affirmatively stated: "There remains therefore a Sabbath rest for the people of God. For the one who has entered His rest has *ceased from his own works*, as God did from His." Hebrews 4:9-10.

The writer of Hebrews says repeatedly that this rest is God's ultimate plan or destiny for His people. This rest is the Glory. The prophet Isaiah, in Chapter 11, speaks of this in verse 10: "Then it will come about in that day that the nations will resort to the root of Jesse, who will stand as a signal for the people, and *His resting place shall be the Glory*." The Church as a whole still has yet to enter it, for the same reason as the Israelites – unbelief, and a refusal to stop focusing on themselves and what God needs to do for them.

In Hebrews 1:3 it is said of Jesus, "And He is *the radiance of His glory* and the exact representation of His nature, and upholds all things by the word of His Power. When He had made purification of sins, *He sat down* at the right hand of the Majesty on high."

Thus in Psalms 110, "The LORD says to my Lord, *sit at My right hand* until I make Thine enemies a footstool for Thy feet." There is a resting place for Jesus at the right hand of the Father, and for us as well, because, according to Ephesians 2:6, God has "*raised us up with Him, and seated us with Him* in the heavenly places, in Christ

Jesus." Paul also states in Col. 3:1-3 "If then you have been raised up with Christ, keep seeking the things above, where Christ is, *seated at the right hand of God*." In other words, seek the resting place where you have already been seated at the right hand of God. Jesus exhorts in Revelation 3:21 "He who overcomes, I will grant to him to sit down with Me on My throne, as I also overcame and sat down with My Father on His throne." Overcomes what, you ask? Overcomes SELF. When we are able to die to self as Jesus did, we will enter the rest He entered, as described in this passage. We will truly experience sitting down on His throne.

According to the Apostle Paul, "For whom He (the Father) foreknew, he also predestined to be *conformed to the image of His Son*, that he might be the first-born among many brethren, and whom He predestined, these He also called, and whom He called, these He also justified, and whom He justified, *these He also glorified*." It is past tense. How (and when) were you glorified? You were "glorified" when you were seated with Christ and given access to the Glory of God the Father. The Glory is your eternal destiny, even though you are not even aware of it. Experiencing the Glory now, here on earth, will propel you into that destiny, will transform you into the image of God's Son, faster than you can even imagine. God is doing a quick work, because these are the last days, and Jesus is coming soon for a spotless, pure Bride – not "Bridezilla" the self-absorbed over-privileged diva insisting on her own way.

His resting place is the Glory (Isaiah 11:10) emanating from the Father at His right hand. If you are focusing entirely on works – ministry, and "building God's kingdom," you are guaranteed to miss the Shabbat, because the Glory is the Shabbat for God's people. This "glory" business is *an offense to those with a "Martha" mentality*, i.e., those who are busy focusing on and working at serving the LORD – especially those who are chasing the anointing and "wanting to move in their giftings" (i.e., selfish ambition and the desire for importance and recognition rather than a sincere desire to serve). By contrast, the resting place that is the Glory is only for the Marys, i.e., those nobodies who are simply sitting with Jesus. (See Luke 10:38-42). The Marthas of today will continue to be offended, bitterly envious, criticizing and even reviling the Marys who have entered into this Glory experience. The Glory is and will always be an offense to works-oriented man-centered activity.

We are conformed (or transformed into) to the image of His Son by beholding the Glory of the Lord (II Corinthians 3:18) in a place of complete cessation of our own works. As Paul says in Colossians 3:3, "You have died, and your life is hidden *with Christ in God.*" When we have died to ourselves, we will be beyond the realm of the anointing, being used by God, laying hands on people, ministering to others, interceding, etc. The Glory is a place only dead people end up, beside Jesus at God's right hand. Jesus said in Matthew 11:28, "come to me all who are weary and heavy laden, and I will give you rest." The place of rest – the atmosphere of the Glory -- is a foretaste of our eternal destiny, which we can experience NOW if we are willing to let go of everything on earth. That means I let go of my ministry, my priorities, my cares and concerns, my desire to be somebody, and all the things I think are so important, and wait upon the LORD – the Father – the God of Israel.

From experience, I can testify that God's glory comes sovereignly to you – the Glory

gradually, silently, gently, almost imperceptibly will
appear, and completely on God's own initiative.
Afterwards you will eventually begin to be aware
you are unable to move, unable to speak, unable
to think or do anything. You will probably feel a
gradually appearing atmosphere of thickness, a
gentle weight, a fog weighing you down, and it
simply crept up on you unawares. You will want
to lie down. You may lose consciousness and then
"come to" minutes or even hours later, wondering
what happened. That's because you didn't create
the atmosphere by anything you did. It's not about
you at all. This isn't the hoopla, the jumping up
and down in the anointing, laying hands on
people, etc. In fact, it is the total opposite. This is
a kind of quiet, intimate experience where you
can't fast it in, you can't pray it in, you can't
worship it in. You simply can't sing loud enough,
holler or groan loud enough, run around the
church building fast enough, or otherwise work up
enough religious activity to experience the Glory.
All you can do is DIE -- *let go*, forget about
yourself – *cease to exist*, and, in the words of Ps.
46:10, "be still, and know that I am God." That is
the true Shabbat – the "Sabbath rest for the
people of God."

CHAPTER 13
THE GLORY AND DOMINION

Psalms 8:3-6 says "When I consider Thy heavens, the work of Thy fingers, the moon and the stars which Thou has ordained, what is man, that Thou dost take thought of him, and the son of man, that Thou dost care for him? Yet Thou has made him a little lower than God (Heb. *Elohim*) and dost crown him with *glory and majesty*." This is the original destiny and purpose for man's creation as expressed by God in Genesis 1:26 "Let Us make man in Our image, according to Our likeness, and let them *have dominion* over the fish of the sea, over the birds of the air, and over the cattle, over *all the earth* and over every creeping thing that creeps on the earth."

The purpose of the Glory is, as previously stated in this book, succinctly expressed in II Corinthians 3:18 "But we all, with unveiled face, beholding as in a mirror the glory of the LORD, are being transformed into the same image from glory to glory." That image and likeness of God – man's original *programming* for dominion – is the "crown of *glory* and majesty," and that original destiny of dominion comes part and parcel with the experience of God's glory.

Paul describes the connection between glory and dominion this way in Romans 8:19-21: "For the anxious longing of the creation waits eagerly for the revealing of the sons of God, for the creation was subjected to futility, not of its own will, but because of Him who subjected it, in hope that the creation itself will be set free from its slavery to corruption *into the freedom of the glory of the children of God.*" Paul goes on later in the chapter to state in v. 28-29 "And we know that *God causes all things to work together for good* to those who love God, to those who are called according to His purpose, for whom He foreknew, He also predestined to become *conformed to the image of His Son*, that He might be the first-born among many brethren." You know that your experience of God's glory is bringing you into this realm of dominion when "all things begin to work together for good" around you – when, incredibly, God begins to directly orchestrate the circumstances in your life to bless you. Why? Because you are being transformed into His image, and the crown of glory and majesty you were originally given at creation becomes increasingly manifested in your life. You become the head and not the tail.

Jesus is the pattern and progenitor of this process of glory and dominion, as expressed in Hebrews 1:7-11: "Thou has made for a little while lower than the angels, Thou has crowned Him with glory and honor, and Thou has appointed Him over the works of Thy hands; Thou has put all things in subjection under His feet. For in subjecting all things to him, He left nothing that is not subject to him. But now we do not yet see all things subjected to Him, But we do see Him who has been made for a little while lower than the angels, namely Jesus, because of the suffering of death *crowned with glory and honor*, that by the grace of God He might taste death for everyone, for it was fitting for Him, for Whom are all things, and through Whom are all things, in *bringing many sons to glory*, to perfect the author of their salvation through sufferings, for both He who sanctifies and those who are sanctified are all from one Father, for which reason *He is not ashamed to call them brethren.*" What these passages are saying is this: the Glory is our destiny, the Father our destination, and dominion our inheritance from God. All of this must begin NOW – not in some future "pie in the sky in the sweet By and By."

Jesus says in Revelation 2:26-29 "And he who overcomes, and he who keeps My deeds until the end, *to him I will give authority over the nations*, and he shall rule them with a rod of iron, as the vessels of the potter are broken to pieces, as I have also received authority from My Father." Jesus states this another way in Matthew 24:44-47 "For this reason, you be ready, too, for the Son of Man is coming at an hour when you do not think He will. Who then is the faithful and sensible slave whom his master *puts in charge* of his household to give them their food at the proper time? Blessed is that slave whom his master finds so doing when He comes. Truly I say to you, that he will *put him in charge* of all his possessions." In other words, you need to be entering into the process of dominion now with Jesus, so that when He returns to earth, He can entrust you with an even greater realm of authority.

This is also the sense of the Parable of the Talents in Matt. 25:23 "His master said to him, well done, good and faithful slave, you were faithful with a few things, I will *put you in charge* of many things, enter into the joy of your master." Thus, we see that this process of overcoming – dying to self, dying even to "my anointing," "my ministry," "my church" and everything else about ME that we value – will enable us to enter God's Shabbat rest through the experience of the Father's Glory. Abiding in the Glory is the key to walking in a process of dominion where we are conformed to the selfless, sacrificial spirit of Christ, and God begins placing things under our feet.

CHAPTER 14
WHOSE CHURCH IS IT ANYWAY?

In order for the Church to access the Glory, we must be willing to die to our own selves, our own "sacred cows," our own cherished personal theological concepts about who we think we know God to be. Only then will we be changed by God's impartation of *Himself – His* values, His ways, His version of reality. Prov. 3:5 says "Trust in the LORD with all your heart, and do not lean on your own understanding." Even more to the point is Isaiah 55:7-9: "Let the wicked forsake his way, and the unrighteous man *his thoughts*, and let him return to the LORD, and He will have compassion on Him, and to our God, for He will abundantly pardon, for *My thoughts are not your thoughts*, neither are your ways My ways, declares the LORD, "For as the heavens are higher than the earth, so are My ways higher than your ways, and my thoughts than your thoughts."

I John 2:27 says "the anointing you have received from Him abides in you, and you have no need for anyone to teach you; but as His anointing teaches you about all things, and is true, and is not a lie, and just as it has taught you, you abide in Him." God will teach us, by experience, how to enter into and abide in the Glory, if we are willing to abandon all preconceived notions and come to him as little children. He has promised a day when "they shall not teach again, each man his neighbor and each man his brother, saying, know the LORD, *for they shall all know Me*, from the least of them to the greatest of them," declares the LORD, "for I will forgive their iniquity, and their sin I will remember no more." Jeremiah 31:34. He also said "I will give them a heart to know Me." Jerermiah24:7. He will also give us His heart for Israel and Jerusalem, and make us passionate for the things he values most.

We are exhorted by Paul in II Thessalonians 5:19 "Quench not the Spirit." What is the biggest obstacle to the Glory in the Church today? It is man-centered activity. If the Church truly wants revival and an experience of God's glory, the *activity of man must cease.* This is not "our church." Jesus said in Matthew 16:18, "Upon this rock I will build <u>My</u> *church."* In that same passage He said to Peter, "Flesh and blood has not revealed this to you, but my Father in heaven." In other words, you may be trying to build *your church* by the effort and ingenuity of "flesh and blood" (man-centered wisdom), but *Jesus is building His Church by the revelation of the Father.* Unless and until we are willing to stop building "our church" and cooperate with Jesus while He builds His, we will not experience the Glory of the Father. It is as simple as that. I recall a statement from a visiting pastor from the underground house church movement in China who visited an American church and told the pastor in genuine awe and amazement, "Wow! I'm so amazed at how much you are able to accomplish without the Holy Spirit!" Having no guile whatsoever and speaking in complete innocence and childlike wonder, he had no idea what a horrible indictment he was making of that church and the American church in general.

Romans 1:21-22 says "For even though they knew God, they did not honor Him as God, or give thanks; but they became futile in their speculations, and their foolish heart was darkened, professing to be wise, they became fools, and exchanged *the glory of the incorruptible God for an image in the form of corruptible man* . . . "This is what is happening in so many American churches today. As long as our church services are man-centered, serving our purposes, addressing our needs, entertaining us and conforming to our image of who we think God is supposed to be, God will continue to give us over to it. We will continue to accomplish amazing things without the Holy Spirit. We will have a form of godliness but little if any real power, and certainly no demonstration of the Glory. But as soon as we decide not to quench the Spirit, as soon as we stop seeking our own gratification, as soon as we are willing to seek God for His own sake, as soon as we are willing to let His glory expose every vile thing about our character and deal with it and die to it – maybe then we will have a real encounter with His Glory like the ex-Muslims do in East Africa. That is my hope and prayer for the Church in America, "as we eagerly wait for a Savior, the Lord Jesus Christ, who will transform the body of our humble state into conformity with the body of His Glory, by the exertion of the power that he has even to subject all things to Himself." Philippians 3:20-21.

BIBLIOGRAPHY

Crann, Alice, "*Pastor orchestrated first revival*", The Pensacola News Journal. November 19, 1997.

Conn, Charles W. *Like A Mighty Army*, Cleveland, Tennessee, Pathway Press, 1994.

Friedman, Dr. Motti, The Pedagogic Center, The Department for Jewish Zionist Education, The Jewish Agency for Israel, (c) 1997, 1998, 1999, 2000, *Jewish Virtual Library*, http://www.jewishvirtuallibrary.org/first-to-twelfth-zionist-congress-1897-1921

Harrell, D. E., *All Things Are Possible: The Healing and Charismatic Revivals in Modern America*, Bloomington, IN, Indiana University Press, 1978.

Johnson, Paul, *A History of the Jews*, New York, New York, Harper Collins, 1987.

Kaplan, Eran, and Penslar, Derek J, *The Origins of Israel 1882-1948, A Documentary History*, Madison, WI, University of Wisconsin Press, 2011.

Laurentin, Rene, *Catholic Pentecostalism*, New York, New York: Doubleday & Company. 1977.

Rabey. Steve, "Fire From Above", *Charisma Magazine*. Lake Mary, Florida, June 2005.

Synan, Vinson. *The Holiness-Pentecostal Tradition*, Grand Rapids, MI, Eerdmans Publishing Co., 1997.

Ward Sr. Mark, *The Electronic Church in the Digital Age: Cultural Impacts of Evangelical Mass Media [2 volumes]: Cultural Impacts of Evangelical Mass Media*, ABC-CLIO, USA, 2015.

RESOURCES

The author recommends the following resources.

Author and ministry website:
www.thechabod.com

Heart For Zion Ministries-Pastors Michael and Sherry Major. Heart for Zion Ministries is a Bible-based Christian Ministry dedicated to teaching the Body of Christ about the Jewish roots of their faith and engendering a heart for Israel in the Christian church.
  We believe that the fullness of God's end-time revelation and true Revival will only come when the Church realizes it is merely a branch grafted into God's cultivated olive tree, Israel.

Music by Michael Major-

Lay It All Down- The worship songs on *Lay it All Down* were recorded live in the studio (in one take!) in early 2001 and were birthed out of Michael's profound 1999 out-of-body experience during worship at the Brownsville Revival. These songs have been used in Michael and Sherry's glory meetings since 2003 to facilitate an atmosphere conducive to the glory.

Glory Encounter- *Glory Encounter* is a collection of 12 original worship songs recorded live at Northern Florida Christian Center in O'Brien, Florida during a special glory service dedicated to intimacy with God and transformation of the Bride of Christ. *Glory Encounter* is designed to be a companion CD in a combined offer with Michael's book.

Dr. Stephen L. Gray-God called Stephen Gray as a faith missionary in July of 1996 to East Africa.

Stephen had no idea of the path God would take him on as a revivalist, pastor, teacher and disciple maker. He is the author of countless discipleship materials and two books called *"The Glory Journal"* and *"Becoming a True Disciple."* He is a seasoned minister of the word of God. He is consumed with making disciples as he has taught hundreds over the years to take up their cross and follow Jesus. He has pastored churches in America and planted churches in Africa. He has served as an elder on Global Fellowship in America and 130 Agape Churches in Africa. He has a PhD from Midwest Seminary in Biblical Studies and Discipleship. As a missionary for 18 years with Stephen Gray Ministries and International Gospel Outreach in Mobile, Alabama he has ministered in Israel, Europe, Africa, Jamaica, Mexico as well as America. Dr. Fred Wolfe formerly of Cottage Hill Baptist church of Mobile Alabama was instrumental in launching Stephen as a missionary over 18 years ago. Dr. Gray offers many resources concerning the glory and discipleship.

Website: http://stephengrayministries.com/

Marie Fowler- All Glorious Within Ministries- Marie Fowler's life was dramatically changed after being discipled in the Glory by Michael and Sherry Major. She serves on the leadership team of Heart for Zion Ministries as an intercessor and is commissioned by Destiny House in Redding, CA. The heart of All Glorious Within Ministries, is to, "Awaken Creation to the glory of God within". After Marie Fowler was marked with transformational encounters the Lord began to pose this question:

Thus says the LORD, "Heaven is My
throne and the earth is My
footstool Where then is a house you
could build for Me? And where is a
place that I may rest? (Isaiah 66:1).

It was this very question that began Marie's search for intimacy and identity with God. This ultimately led to the revelation of habitation and the 12 Tribes of Israel in her book *Living Stones*. Marie Fowler is an Ambassador of Identity whose passion is to build God's house within the context of family. All Glorious Within Ministries offers a unique discipleship program within the context of the revelation found in *Living Stones*. This program is offered both online and in thriving worship community houses.

Website: www.allgloriouswithin.com

www.ingramcontent.com/pod-product-compliance
Lightning Source LLC
Chambersburg PA
CBHW060051050426
42448CB00011B/2405